Preface

The fields of Database Management Systems (DBMS) represent a cornerstone of modern computing, serving as the backbone for data storage, retrieval, and management across various industries. As organizations increasingly rely on data-driven decision-making, the significance of robust database management cannot be overstated. Recognizing this importance, the Indira Gandhi National Open University (IGNOU) has integrated Database Management Systems into its curriculum, challenging students to master both theoretical foundations and practical applications.

This book, IGNOU Introduction to Database Management Systems (MCS-203) Previous Years Unsolved Papers, is a thoughtfully curated compilation of unsolved question papers from previous years. It is designed to be an indispensable resource for students preparing for their exams in this subject. The primary objective of this book is to provide students with a comprehensive tool to self-assess their understanding, identify areas for improvement, and refine their problem-solving skills.

We believe that practicing with previous years' question papers is one of the most effective strategies for exam preparation. It not only familiarizes students with the types and formats of questions they are likely to encounter but also deepens their understanding of the subject matter by applying concepts to real-world scenarios. By working through these unsolved papers, students will be able to gauge their readiness, enhance their time management during exams, and build confidence in tackling challenging questions.

The decision to present these papers unsolved was deliberate. We encourage students to engage actively with the material, think critically, and explore various approaches to solving the problems. This method fosters independent learning and ensures that students are well-prepared to adapt to diverse question formats and complexities during their actual exams.

This book covers a broad spectrum of topics within Database Management Systems, including relational models, SQL, database design, normalization, transaction management, and security issues. Each paper has been meticulously selected to ensure comprehensive coverage of the syllabus, providing students with a thorough understanding of the core concepts essential for success in their exams.

We hope that this book will not only assist students in their academic journey but also inspire them to explore the exciting world of database management systems further. As data continues to play a pivotal role in shaping the future, the knowledge and skills acquired in Database Management Systems will undoubtedly be invaluable.

We would like to extend our sincere gratitude to the faculty members and students of IGNOU who have contributed to the development of this book. Your feedback and insights have been instrumental in ensuring that this book meets the needs of today's learners.

Wishing you success in your studies and your future endeavours in the world of Database Management Systems.

Table of Contents

MCA (Revised)
Chapter 1: Term-End Examination, June, 2010
MCS-023: Database Management Systems

Time: 3 Hours
Maximum Marks: 100
Weightage: 70

Note: (i) Question No. 1 is compulsory.
(ii) Answer any three Questions from the rest.

Q1. (a) Define 3 NF. Justify whether the following relation satisfies 3 NF or not? In case it does not, decompose it into relations which do satisfy 3 NF. What advantages are gained by this decomposition? 2+5+1=8

Roll No.	Name	Department	Year	Hostel Name
R1	N1	D1	1	H1
R2	N2	D2	1	H1
R3	N3	D1	2	H2
R4	N4	D2	2	H2
R5	N5	D1	3	H3
R6	N6	D3	4	H4

(b) Consider the following tables : 15
Working (P_name, C_name, Salary)
Living (P_name, Street, City)
Located (C_name, city)
When P_name = Professor name,
C-name = College name.
Write the SQL Queries for the following.
1. List the names and cities they live in, of the professors who are working for the college C1
2. Find the name, street and city of the professors who are working for the college C2 and are having a salary more than 60000/-.
3. Find the names of professors who live and work in the same city.
4. Find the names of the professors who do not work for college C3.
5. Find the professors whose salaries are less than that of all of the college C4 employees.
6. Display college wise total salary.

(c) Explain the concept of data independence. 3

(d) List and explain all the types of constraints which can be violated while modifying database values. 6

(e) What is a weak entity? Explain with the help of an example. 1+2

(f) Explain the hash file - organisation with the help of a suitable diagram. What are its shortcomings. 5

Q2. (a) For the following statement, draw an E-R diagram. Make and state any reasonable assumptions. "A machine shop produces many parts which it takes on contract. It employs many operators who operate any of the machines. A part is produced using only one machine. A record is kept on the quantity of material needed for producing each part. The production of each part is tracked by giving a job number, start time and end time and operator's identification". 8

(b) What is a transaction? Describe the ACID properties of transaction. 1+4

(c) What is a deadlock. Explain the schemes of deadlock prevention. 1+4

(d) Define the term DML pre-compiler. 2

Q3. (a) Differentiate between the followings: 12
(i). 2 Tier and 3 Tier architecture
(ii). Equi join and Natural join
(iii). Global and local transaction
(iv). Procedural and Non-Procedural DMLs.

(b) What is Cartesian product. Explain using an example. How Cartesian product operation is related to the join operation.
4

(c) Consider the relations 4
student (d name, address)
marks (id, course, marks)
Create an authorization matrix for two users Viz. Student and Administrator. Make and state suitable assumptions.

Q4. Explain the following with the help of an example / diagram wherever needed: 20
(a) Conditions of occurrence of deadlocks
(b) Primary and Secondary indexes
(c) BCNF
(d) Two phase locking

Q5 (a) What is log based recovery ? Explain by taking an example of concurrent transactions. What are its drawbacks.
2+5+1

(b) Why do we need to fragment a relation ? What are the rules to be followed during fragmentation.
6

(c) Explain the following relational algebraic operations with the help of an example. 6
(i). Division operator
(ii). Set Difference operator

MCA (Revised)
Chapter 2: Term-End Examination, December, 2010
MCS-023: Database Management Systems

Time: 3 Hours
Maximum Marks: 100
Weightage: 70

Note: (i) Question No. 1 is compulsory.
(ii) Answer any three Questions from the rest.

Q1. (a) State the two integrity rules. Also explain through an example when these two rules are violated?
2+2

(b) Define 2NF. Justify whether the following "Products" relation is in 2NF or not. In case it does not satisfy 2NF, decompose it into a set of relations which do satisfy 2NF. What advantages are gained by this decomposition Products Relation.
2+5+1

Brand Name	Size	Price	Manufacturer
B1	L	P1	MF1
B1	E	P2	MF1
B1	E	P3	MF1
B2	E	P4	MF1
B3	E	P5	MF2
B3	L	P6	MF2

(c) Consider the following database schema: 10
Student (Name, Student Number, Class, Major)
Course (Course Name, Course Number Credit Hours, Department)
Section (Section ID, Course Number, Semester, Year, professor)
Grade-Report (Student Number, Section ID, Grade)
Prerequisite (Course Number, Prerequisite Number)

Specify the following question using SQL
(i) Retrieve the names of all students majoring in CS
(ii) Retrieve the names of all courses taught by professor P1 in the years 2000 and 2001
(iii) Retrieve the name and transcript (Course Name, course Number, Credit Hours, Semester, Year and Grade) of each student majoring in CS Assis
(iv) Retrieve the names and major of all student who have a grade A in atleast one course.
(v) Retreive the names and major departments of all students who do not have a A grade in any of their Courses

(d) List all the four types of constraints which may be violated while inserting a new record into a relation. Explain through an example. 2+4

(e) What are Sparse and dense indexes? 2+2

(f) What is the two phase locking protocol? How does it guarantee Serializability Explain 2+3

(g) Define the following terms: 3
(i). Concurrency
(ii). Data Dictionary

2. (a) Draw an E-R Diagram for the following statements. Make and state any reasonable assumptions.

"Dr X is Starting a medical practice. He wants a Computerized system to manage the appointments, maintain patients records and generate reports. When a patient calls for an appointment, the receptionist checks the schedule and fixes the appointment at the earlier date. The receptionist enters the appointment with patient's name, purpose of appointment and the date of appointment agreed upon, the system verifies the patients name and supplies the necessary details from the patient's record. The system should also print weekly schedule"
10

(b) Explain the B-Tree index with the help of a diagram. What are the advantages of using B-Tree indexes? 5

(c) Construct an example for each of the following relational algebraic operations: 5
(i) Select
(ii) Project
(iii) Cartesian product
(iv) Union
(v) Join

3. Differentiate between the following. 20
(i) Backward recovery and Forward recovery
(ii) Horizontal and vertical fragmentation
(iii) outer join and Self join
(iv) Serial schedule and serializable schedule
(v) 3NF and BCNF

4. (a) Write and explain the following schemes in order to prevent deadlock. 6
(i). wait die scheme
(ii). would-wait scheme

(b) What are the problems which may occur when transactions are executed concurrently. Explain each of them with the help of an example. 8

(c) Write all the steps for distributed database 2+4 design and explain. 2+4

Q5. (a) What are the differences among primary, secondary and clustering indexes? Explain these with the help of suitable example. List the issues in implementation of each of these indexes. 10

(b) Explain the terms transaction roll back and credit roll back. 4

(c) When the decomposition of a relation is lossy? Explain with the help an example. 3+3

MCA (Revised)

Chapter 3: Term-End Examination, June, 2011

MCS-023: Database Management Systems

Time: 3 Hours
Maximum Marks: 100
Weightage: 70

Note: (i) Question No. 1 is compulsory.
(ii) Answer any three Questions from the rest.

1. (a) Explain following operators in Relational Algebra with the help of an example 5
(i) Select
(ii) Project
(iii) Join

(b) Analyse the following relations. Child (C-name, C-age, C-address) Parent (P-name, P-age, C-name, C-age) and identify the highest normal form possessed by them. If the relation is desired to be normalized then perform the task, otherwise justify with suitable arguments that "Normalization is not needed". 6

(c) What are the advantages of using B tree as a structure for creating index ? 5

(d) A concurrent schedule of transactions T1 and T2 acting on "SUM" is given below : 6

Schedule	**T1**	**T2**	**Sum**
-	-	-	100
$Read_1$ (Sum)	$Read_1$ (Sum)		
Sum = Sum + 10	Sum = Sum + 10		
$Read_2$ (Sum)		$Read_2$ (Sum)	
$Write_1$ (Sum)	$Write_1$ (Sum)		
Sum = Sum - 10		Sum = Sum - 10	
$Write_1$ (Sum)		$Write_2$ (Sum)	

Analyzing the given concurrent schedule performing following tasks.
(i) What is the final value of "SUM" ?
(ii) Verify that the given schedule is serializable or not. Explain.

(e) Explain log based recovery scheme with the help of an example. 6

(f) How client server databases differs from Distributed Databases ? Explain with the help of an example. 6

(g) Define Functional Dependency (FD). Find 6 the valid FD's in the following relation. 6

A	**B**	**C**	**D**
a_1	b_1	c_1	d_1
a_2	b_2	c_2	d_2

a_3	b_2	c_3	d_3
a_4	b_3	c_4	d_4

2. (a) Is it always beneficial to work with database systems, or some times filebase system is a better option ? Comment on it with suitable arguments. 3

(b) Explain physical data independence and logical data independence. 4

(c) Determine the output when following operations are applied on relations R1, R2 and R3 given below. 7

For R_1:

A	B
A_1	B_1
A_2	B_2
A_3	B_3
A_4	B_4

For R_2:

X	Y
A_1	B_1
A_7	B_7
A_2	B_2
A_4	B_4

For R_3:

A
empty

(i) Union (R1 U R2)
(ii) Intersection (R1 ∩ R2)
(iii) Difference (R1 — R2)
(iv) Cartesian cross - section (R1 x R2)
(v) Division (R1 / R3)
(d) Draw E.R Diagram for the statement given below. 6

Note : Use suitable notations at appropriate places.
"Many teachers teaches many students in many institutes affiliated to many Universities, the institutes are categorised as
Engineering, Medical and Management institutes".

3. (a) What do you mean by integrity constraints ? Briefly describe the various types of integrity constraints. 4
(b) Explain insert, delete and update anomalies for a relation (R), with examples. 6
(c) An ordered employee file (ordering field is emp_id) has 20000 records, stored on a disk having block size 1k. Assume that each student record is of 100 bytes, the ordering field is of 8 bytes and block pointer is also of 8 bytes, find how many block accesses on average may be saved on using primary index. 7
(d) List the desirable properties of decomposition of a data base. 3

4. (a) Write SQL statements to perform following queries on the given relations i.e. 8
Employee (Empid, Emp_name, Dept_id)
Department (Dept_id, Dept_name,
Dept_loc, Emp_id)
(i) List the names of employees whose name starts with 'S'

(ii) To sort the employee data, in the alphabetic descending order.
(iii) Find total number of employees.
(iv) Find the department number and number of employees working in each department.

(b) Explain 2 phase locking protocol. 4
(c) What is a transaction ? Briefly describe the properties of the transactions. 4
(d) Describe the following : 4
(i) Optimistic scheduling
(ii) Disadvantages of SQL

5. (a) With the help of suitable example discuss the utility of check points in Database recovery. 6
(b) Explain the horizontal and vertical data fragmentation, with examples. 6
(c) Explain the following : 6
(i) Data Replication
(ii) 2-Tier Client/Server model
(d) List any four responsibilities of DBA. 2

MCA (Revised)
Chapter 4: Term-End Examination, June, 2012
MCS-023: Database Management Systems

Time: 3 Hours
Maximum Marks: 100
Weightage: 70

Note: (i) Question No. 1 is compulsory.
(ii) Answer any three Questions from the rest.

1. (a) Explain the role of the following components of Database Management System. 6
(i) Transaction Manager
(ii) Query Processor
(iii) Storage Manager

(b) Consider the following relation schemas R = (A, B, C) and S = (D, E, F) with r an s be the corresponding relations respectively. Give an expression in SQL for the following queries : 4
(i) $\pi A(R)$
(ii) $\sigma(B=17)^{(r)}$
(iii) r x s
(iv) π A, F ($\sigma_{C=D}$ (rxs))

(c) Define primary key, candidate key, super key and foreign key 4

(d) Decompose the relation R = (A, B, C, D, E) with the set of functional dependencies 4
(i). A —> BC
(ii). CD --> E
(iii). B —> D into 3NF relation

(e) What are the functions of a Database Administrator. 5

(f) Justify the following statements 6
(i) Two phase locking leads to serializability schedules.
(ii) A Relation in BCNF is also in 3NF.

(g) Discuss the problems associated with concurrent transactions. 6

(h) Write down the advantages and disadvantages of distributed DBMS. 5

2. For the following problem definition :
The book club has members. The book club sells books to its members. The members places orders for books, which the book club fulfils. Each order contains one or more than one books. The books are written by author (s). The publisher publishes the book. An author can write more than one book and a book can have more than one author. A book is published by a publisher, but a publisher publishes many books. A member can place more than one order. The member also can choose not to place an order. The book club sells many books.
(a) Draw an E - R Diagram 10
(b) Map the ER Diagram to Relational model. 10

3. (a) Consider the following Tables : 16
Works (Pname, Cname, salary)
LIVES (Pname, street, city)
LOCATED (Cname, city)

MANAGER (Pname, Mname)
Write queries in SQL for the following
(i) List the names of the people who work for the company Wipro along with the cities they live in.
(ii) Find the people who work for the company 'Infosys' having salary greater than Rs - 50000/-
(iii) List the names of the people, along with the street and city addresses.
(iv) Find the persons whose salaries are more than that of all of the 'Oracle' employees.
(v) And the name of the persons who do not work in 'Infosys'.
(vi) Find the average salary of the employee in company named `accenture'.
(vii) Create a table for the above relation using SQL - DDL
(viii) Create a view consisting of the person name along with their manager name and company name.

(b) What are the problems caused by deadlock ? Give a Mechanism to detect deadlock .4

4. (a) Explain the purpose of check points in database recovery. 4

(b) Why is a B tree a better structure than a binary search tree for implementation of an index ? 5

(c) Explain the log based recovery in Database systems. 5

(d) Consider the relation R (A, B, C, D, E) and the set of functional dependencies :-
F(A —>D,{A,B} D —> E)
(i) Which of the following are candidate keys ?
(A) (Al
(B) (A, B}
(C) {A, El
(ii) Consider the decomposition of R into {R1 (A, B, C) and R2 (A, D, E)}. Is this decomposition lossless ? Justify ? 6

5. (a) Discuss the measures that are used to provide security of data in databases. 5

(b) What is a fragment of a relation ? What are the main types of fragments ? Why is fragmentation used in distributed Database Design ? 5
(c) Discuss the different states of a Transaction with the help of a diagram. 4
(d) Explain the following terms : 6
(i) Secondary Index
(ii) Data Dictionary
(iii) Division operation in Relational Algebra.

MCA (Revised)
Chapter 5: Term-End Examination, December,2012
MCS-023: Database Management Systems

Time: 3 Hours
Maximum Marks: 100
Weightage: 70

Note: (i) Question No. 1 is compulsory.
(ii) Answer any three Questions from the rest.

1. (a) Design ER Diagram for the following statement : 10
"Each Bank can have multiple branches and each branch can have multiple accounts and loans". Convert the ER diagram into relational model (i.e. tables). Identify the keys and describe the integrity constraints.

(b) How would you normalize EMP-DEPT in to 3NF? EMP-DEPT(ENAME, SSN, BDATE, ADDRESS, DNUMBER, DNAME, DMGRSSN) Where following dependencies are given SSN ---> ENAME, BDATE, ADDRESS, DNUMBER DNUMBER --> DNAME, DMGRSSN.
10

(c) Consider the relation R(A,B,C,D) with the following dependencies : 5
AB --> C, CD ---> E,DE --->B is AB a candidate key of this relation ? Explain your answer.

(d) What is a system log? What are the typical kind on entries in a system catalog? 5

(e) Draw diagram to show the states of transaction execution. Briefly discuss each of the states, shown in the diagram.
5

(f) Draw the block diagram to show the components of Database manager. 5

2. (a) Consider the relation R(A,B,C,D,E,F,G,H) with functional dependency set as FD = {A C; B CG; AD EH; C DF; A—>H} On the basis of the given details, perform following tasks. 4+6=10
(i) Determine key for relation R
(ii) Decompose R into 2NF, 3NF and finally in BCNF.

(b) Compare primary, secondary and clustering Indexes. Which of these indexes are dense and which are not ? How is implementation of clustering indexes performed ? 6+2+2=10

3. (a) What do you mean by the terms "Loss-Less Decomposition" and "Dependency Preserving Decomposition" ?
5

(b) What problems occur in the database when transactions do not satisfy ACID properties ? Explain explicitly using suitable
examples ? 7

(c) Consider the following relations : 2x4=8

P: Pid	Pname	Q : Pid	Pname
001	abc	012	xyz
012	xyz	014	lmn
014	lmn	016	SSS
015	opq	017	SSD
017	SSD		

Find the following :
(i) Pu Q (ii) P— Q

(iii) P n Q (iv) P x Q

4. (a) What do you mean by Integrity constraints ? Briefly discuss, the different type of integrity constraints. 5

(b) What do you mean by the term "database recovery"? Explain any two recovery techniques. 7

(c) Compare and contrast the following (Any two) : 8
(i) Wait and die And Wait and wound protocol
(ii) Physical data independence and Logical data independence
(iii) Centralized and Distributed DBMS

5. (a) What are the advantages of DDBMS over centralized DBMS ? Why is data replication and fragmentation performed in DDBMS ? What typical units of data are replicated ? 10

(b) What is two phase locking protocol ? How does it guarantee serializability? Explain. 5

(c) Discuss the multiversion technique for concurrency control. 5

MCA (Revised)
Chapter 6: Term-End Examination, June, 2013
MCS-023: Database Management Systems

Time: 3 Hours
Maximum Marks: 100
Weightage: 70

Note: (i) Question No. 1 is compulsory.
(ii) Answer any three Questions from the rest.

1. (a) Discuss the difference between database systems and file Based systems. 5

(b) Explain the GROUPBY clause. What is the difference between the WHERE and HAVING clause in SQL ? 6

(c) Define foreign key. Explain its significance. 4

(d) Is BCNF stronger than SNF ? Justify your answer with the help of an example. 5

(e) Discuss the different process of authorisation permitted on database items with the help of examples ? 6

(f) Define Data Independence ? Explain the difference between physical and logical data independence. 5

(g) List all the functional dependencies that holds true for the following relation. 4

A	B	C
a_1	b_1	c_1
a_1	b_1	c_2
a_2	b_1	c_1
a_2	b_1	c_3

(h) Discuss the two-phase locking protocol in concurrency control ? 5

2. (a) Construct on E-R diagram for the following problem definition: 8
Each company operates four departments, and each department belongs to one company. Each department employs one
or more employees, and each employee works for one department. Each of the employees may or may not have one or more
dependents, and each dependent belongs to one employee.

(b) Explain Generalisation/Specialisation in an E-R diagram with the help of an example ? 6

(c) How would you map the following ER constructs into relations ? Give suitable example. 6
(i) Weak Entity

(ii) Generalization
(iii) Ternary Relationship.

3. (a) What is an outer join ? Discuss the different 5 types of outer joins with the help of example.

(b) Consider the following relations for a database that keeps track of business trips of salespersons in a sales office: SALES PERSON (SSN, Name, Start-Year, Dept-No) TRIP(SSN, From-City, To-City, Departure- Date, Return-Date, Trip-ID) EXPENSE(Trip-ID, Account #, Amount) Specify the following queries in SQL? 9
(i) Find the details (all attributes of TRIP relation) for trips whose expenses exceeds $2000.
(ii) Find the SSN of salesman who took trips to 'Honolulu'.
(iii) Find the total trip expenses incurred by the salesman with
SSN = '234 — 56 — 7890'.
(iv) Write the DDL expressions for the above relations:

(c) Define a view ? How is it different from a table ? Write the SQL Syntax for creating a view. 6

(b) What are the differences between BST-Tree and B tree Indexes ? 4

(c) Compare sequential file organisation with Heap files organisation. Discuss the advantages and disadvantages of sequential file organisation. 5

(d) Explain the following terms : 6
(i) Equi Join
(ii) Data Replication
(iii) Entity Integrity Constraints.

4. (a) Consider the following relation for published books : 10
Book (Book title, Author name, Book-type, list price, Author-affil, Publisher) (Author-affil referes to the affiliation of the
author.) Suppose the following dependencies exist :
Book-title →Publisher, Book-type
Book-type y → list price
Author-name → Author-affil
(i) What normal form is the above relation in ? Justify.
(ii) Normalize the above relation to its highest Normal form.
(b) Discuss the different types of fragmentation in distributed databases with the help of an example. 5
(c) Explain the ACID properties of transactions in Database system. 5

5. (a) Consider the precedence graph of a schedule given below. Is the schedule serializable ? Justify. 5

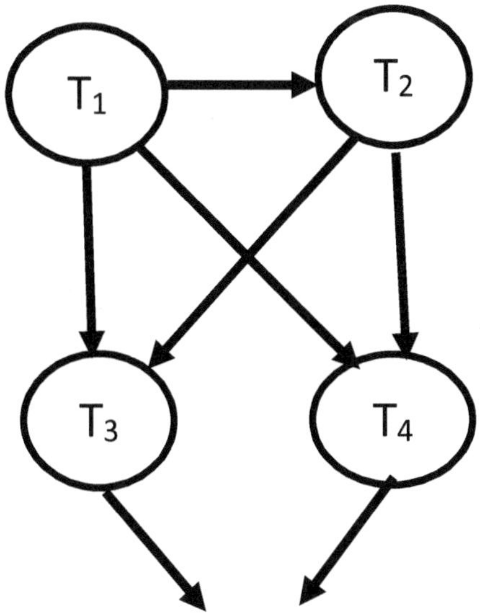

T_5

MCA (Revised)
Chapter 7: Term-End Examination, December,2013
MCS-023: Database Management Systems

Time: 3 Hours
Maximum Marks: 100
Weightage: 70

Note: (i) Question No. 1 is compulsory.
(ii) Answer any three Questions from the rest.

1. (a) Consider the following relations : 2.5x4=10
hotel (hotel no, hotel name, city) room (room no, hotel no, type, price) booking (hotel no guest no, date from, date to, room no) guest (guest no, g name, g address) Write appropriate Queries in SQL as well as in relational algebra, for the following :
(i) Find the average price of a room
(ii) List the names and address of all guests with bookings for a hotel in London, alphabetically ordered by name.
(iii) Find the total income from all the rooms of the hotels in New York
(v) List the name(s) of guest(s) at the Winner. Hotel, who are paying highest price for a room.
(b) Differentiate between BCNF and 3NF. Why BCNF is considered as a stronger form of 3NF ? 7

(c) Briefly discuss the concept of catalogs in distributed databases. How catalogs are used to maintain the consistency of database in an distributed environment. Use suitable example to justify your answer. 8

(d) Design an ER diagram for keeping track of the details of your favourite sports team. You should stone the matches played, the score in each match and individual player statistics for each match. Identify the entities, relationships and also mention the cardinality of ER diagram. 8

(e) List all the functional dependencies satisfied by the relational instance given below : 7

A	B	C
a_1	b_1	c_1
a_1	b_1	c_2
a_1	b_1	c_1
a_2	b_1	c_3

2. (a) Draw block diagram of ANSI SPARC 3 Level architecture. Mention following in the diagram : 8

(i) Languages used at each level.
(ii) Data independence types, between different levels.
(iii) SQL commands, associated with the languages used at each level.

(b) How serial schedule is different from serializable schedule ? What are the problems associated with both schedules ? How you will identify that a schedule is serializable ornot, use suitable example, in support of your answer. 7

(c) What are the additional functions does a distributed DBMS have over centralized DBMS? 5

3. (a) Describe the shadow paging recovery technique. Under what circumstances does it not require a log ? 5

(b) What is a view in SQL ? How is it defined ? Discuss the problems that may arise when one attempts to update a view. 7

(c) What is the difference between centralized and client-server architectures ? How relational DBMS is evolved from the centralized architecture to the client server architecture ? What for ODBC is used in this context ? 8

4. Discuss the differences between serial, hashed and indexed sequential file organizations. Compare their storage and access efficiencies. 8

(b) What is optimistic scheduling ? Explain the 5 three phases of optimistic scheduling. 8

(c) Why do we normalize a database ? Write statement of 21\1F. Briefly discuss the insert, delete and update anomalies, if the relation is not in 2NF. 7

5. (a) Write short notes on following (Any two) 7
(i) 2 - Phase locking
(ii) 2 - Phase commit
(iii) Time stamping

(b) What do you mean by the term "TRANSACTION" in DBMS ? Briefly discuss the properties of transaction ? Violation of which property leads to which problem, when transactors are executed in an concurrent environment. 8

(c) What is a check point ? How is the check point information used in recovery operation, following a system crash ? 8

MCA (Revised)
Chapter 8: Term-End Examination, June, 2014
MCS-023: Database Management Systems

Time: 3 Hours
Maximum Marks: 100
Weightage: 70

Note: (i) Question No. 1 is compulsory.
(ii) Answer any three Questions from the rest.

1. (a) What is a join in DBMS ? Explain three types of join with the help of an example for each. 7

(b) What is data independence ? Explain two types of data independence with the help of an example for each. 7

(c) What is DDL ? How it is different from DML ? Briefly explain guidelines for creation of table. 6

(d) Explain distributed transaction with the help of an example. 5

(e) What are integrity constraints ? Explain two types of integrity constraint with the help of an example. 5

(f) What is Functional Dependency (FD) ? Find the valid FD's in the following relation : 5

A	B	C
i	1	2
i	1	3
j	1	4
j	1	3
k	2	5
l	4	7

(g) Explain briefly advantages and disadvantages of Distributed Database Management Systems. 5

2. (a) Draw an ER diagram for the situation given below : 8
Library consists of many books in different subject areas where books are written by different authors and are published by
different publishers. A book is published by only one publisher. There are inside - members and outside – members who gets books issued for their uses. The issuing and return operation of the books are managed by the librarian.

(b) What is database recovery ? Explain with an example, how system log is used for database recovery. 5

(c) Explain 3NF. Also justify the statement "BCNF is stronger than 3NF" with the help of an example. 7

3. (a) Explain ANSI SPARC 3 - Level Architecture of DBMS, with the details of languages associated at different levels and the type of data independence involved in between different levels. 6

(b) What is the need of Indexing in DBMS ? Explain the significance of primary Index with the help of an example. 7

(c) What is data redundancy in DBMS ? How data redundancies are removed ? Explain whether the following relation named student is in 2NF or not with proper justification. STUDENT (Name, Course, Age, Sex) 7

4. (a) What is Data Fragmentation ? Explain differences between Horizontal Fragmentation and vertical Fragmentation with the help of suitable example of each. 7

(b) What are nested queries ? explain with the help of an example. 5

(c) Consider the following relations 8
STUDENT (Name, Roll_Number, Teacher_ID, Programme, Semester, Subject) DEPARTMENT (Dep_ID, Programme,
Teacher_ID) TEACHER(Teacher_ID,Dep_ID, Name, Subject)
Write the following queries using SQL :
(i) List name of all the teachers who belong to Dep_ID ='4' and take "Graph Theory", subject.
(ii) List names of all the students who study in Semester-II of BCA programme and are taught by Teacher_ID = '1'.
(iii) Find the name of all the teachers who teaches to the student whose ROLL Number ='101'.
(iv) Find the name of all the students who are in Is' semester of MCA programme and are taught by Prof. Ajay.

5. (a) A file has r = 10,000 Bank Account records of fixed length. Each record has the following fields :
Name (20 bytes), Account_No(8 bytes), address (40 bytes), Balance (15 bytes) and Branch-Code (5 bytes). The file is stored on a disk with the following characteristics : Block Size = 512 bytes, Inter Block Gap = 128 bytes, number of block per track = 15, Number of tracks per sector = 300. A disk pack consist of double side disks. 15
(i) Calculate record size R in bytes.
(ii) Calculate the blocking factor (bfr) and the number of file blocks b, assuming an unspanned organization.
(iii) Calculate the average time it takes to find a record doing a linear search on the file , in which file blocks are not stored contiguously.
(iv) Assume that the file is ordered by "Branch-Code", calculate the time it takes to search for a record given its "Branch_Code", by using a binary search..

(b) Write short note on the following 10
(i) Concurrency Control
(ii) Database Views

MCA (Revised)
Chapter 9: Term-End Examination, December,2014
MCS-023: Database Management Systems

Time: 3 Hours
Maximum Marks: 100
Weightage: 70

Note: (i) Question No. 1 is compulsory.
(ii) Answer any three Questions from the rest.

1. (a) What is SQL ? Explain its important features. 6

(b) Let the transactions T1, T2 and T3 be defined to perform the following operations : 6
T1 : Double A,
T2 : Add 2 to A,
T3 : Display A on screen and set A to 5.
If the transactions T1, T2 and T3 are allowed to execute concurrently, and A is initialized to value 1, then how many possible correct results are there ? Enumerate them.

(c) What is distributed DBMS ? List the issues involved in the design of a distributed DBMS. Also explain the features of
distributed transaction with the help of an example. 8

(d) Determine the output when the following operations are applied on relations R1, R2 and R3 given below :
8

For R_1:

A	B
A_1	B_1
A_2	B_2
A_3	B_3
A_4	B_4

For R_2:

X	Y
A_1	B_1
A_7	B_7
A_2	B_2
A_4	B_4

For R_3:

A
empty

(i) Union (R1 U R3)
(ii) Intersection (R1 ∩ R2)
(iii) Cartesian cross-section (R1 x R2)
(iv) Difference (R2 — R1)
(vi) Division (R1 / R3)

(e) What is a checkpoint ? Briefly explain its importance. 5

(f) Prove the statement, "Any relation which is in BCNF is in 3NF but the converse is not true." 5

(g) List any four responsibilities of a DBA. 2

2. (a) Explain Two-phase locking protocol with an example. 5

(b) What is data integrity ? Does data integrity have any relationship with data security ? Justify- your answer with the
help of example and diagram. 7

(c) What do you mean by fragmentation of a database ? What is the need of fragmentation in DDBMS environment ? Explain different types of fragmentation with an example of each. 8

3. (a) What is the role of Indexing in file organization ? Explain the following in relation to file organization, with the help
of an example for each : 10

(i) Primary Index
(ii) Secondary Index
(iii) Multilevel Indexing

(b) Draw an E-R Diagram for the situation given below : 10

An organization needs to provide Medical facilities to its employees and their dependents. Organization is having a list of
Doctors, Hospitals and Test centres for the employees facility. An employee may get Medical facility from the list of Doctors,
Hospitals and Test centres provided by the organization to them. Employee does not need to pay anything for the facilities
availed. The Doctors, Hospitals and Test centres directly raise their bill to the organization.

Note : Make necessary assumptions wherever required for making E-R Diagram. Show clearly weak and strong entities and their relation in the system.

4. (a) What is Functional Dependency ? Explain single-valued dependency with an example. 5

(b) Explain Physical DBMS architecture with the help of a diagram. 7

(c) Explain the following in brief : 8

(i) Client-Server Databases
(ii) Log-based recovery

5. (a) Explain the following with the help of an example : 8

(i) Loss-less decomposition of database
(ii) Deadlock and its prevention in database system

(b) Write SQL statements to perform the following queries on the relations given below :

BOOK (Book_ID, Title, Publisher_ID, Year_of Pub, Price)
AUTHOR (Author_ID, Book_ID, Author Name)
PUBLISHER (Publisher_ID, Book_ID, Address, Name_of Pub, No._of Copies)

(i) Find the name of authors whose books are published by "ABC Press".
(ii) Find the name of the author and price of the book, whose Book_ID is '100'.
(iii) Find the title of the books which are published by Publisher_ID '20' and are published in year 2011.
(iv) Find the address of the publisher who has published Book_ID "500".

(c) Explain the effect of a rollback operation with an example. 4

MCA (Revised)
Chapter 10: Term-End Examination, June, 2015
MCS-023: Database Management Systems

Time: 3 Hours
Maximum Marks: 100
Weightage: 70

Note: (i) Question No. 1 is compulsory.
(ii) Answer any three Questions from the rest.

1. (a) Give the limitations of file based system. How can they be overcome using DBMS ? 7

(b) Discuss the 3-level architecture of DBMS. Explain how it leads to data independence. 8

(c) A bookshop has a huge collection of books to sell them online and therefore requires a database to track its sales. For each book they store the Title, Author(s) • name, Publisher, Volume, ISBN No., Price, Stock (no. of copies), Year of publication, etc. To help the customers to search the book, they require that each book is assigned to one or more categories such as Engineering, Sciences, Fiction, Literature, Applications, etc. If at all, any discounts that are there for certain books, need to be notified on the site (best-buy offer). To buy a book, a customer needs to register on the site. Also it maintains the profile of the user and also their earlier purchases. The bookshop also sends "Newsletter" to all the registered users to update them about the publications. Identify the entities, relationships, constraints and cardinality and construct an ER diagram for the above mentioned specifications.
10

(d) Discuss briefly about Sparse and Dense Indexes with the help of an example. 10

(e) What is a view ? What are the major advantages of views ? Explain with the help of an example.
5

2. (a) Discuss the use of B-Tree as a structure for creating index, with the help of an example in support.
10

(b) Explain the Log-based recovery scheme with the help of an example. 6

(c) Explain 2-phase locking protocol. 4

3. (a) Consider the following relation EMP. Create queries for it : 10

empno	ename	job	sal	depno
116	NAND	Manager	29,750	40
118	KAPOOR	Analyst	30,000	10
119	HARISH	President	50,000	20
112	ANAND	Analyst	30,000	20
115	BOBBY	Clerk	15,000	20

(i) Get details of employee having minimum salary (sal).
(ii) Display employee whose job title (job) is same as that of employee 116 and sal > sal of employee 118.
(iii) Find average sal.
(iv) Find the ename, depno, sal of employee drawing maximum sal.

(b) Explain the data models, used to structure the data in the database systems. 10

4. (a) Explain the need of Distributed DBMS over Centralized DBMS. Also give the structure of Distributed DBMS. 10

(b) List and explain the 4 basic properties of a Transaction with the help of appropriate examples. 10

5. Write short notes on the following : 4x5=20
(a) Locks
(b) Deadlock and its prevention
(c) Database Errors
(d) Data fragmentation in Distributed databases

MCA (Revised)
Chapter 11: Term-End Examination, December,2015
MCS-023: Database Management Systems

Time: 3 Hours
Maximum Marks: 100
Weightage: 70

Note: (i) Question No. 1 is compulsory.
(ii) Answer any three Questions from the rest.

1. (a) With the help of a neat diagram, explain the physical DBMS architecture. 10

(b) With the help of an appropriate example for each, explain the following basic set operations : 10
(i) UNION
(ii) INTERJECTION
(iii) SET DIFFERENCE
(iv) CARTESIAN PRODUCT

(c) Design an ER diagram for the specifications to maintain any IGNOU's study centre. Clearly indicate the entities, attributes, constraints, relationships and the cardinality. 10

(d) Differentiate between Horizontal fragmentation and Vertical fragmentation with the help of suitable examples in Data
fragmentation of Distributed databases. 10

2. (a) Explain the Sequential file organization. Give the advantages and disadvantages of it. 10

(b) Write in detail about B-Tree structure for indexes with a neat diagram. 10

3. (a) Explain "Write Ahead Log Protocol" with suitable example / diagram. 5

(b) Explain in detail the mechanism of Optimistic Concurrency Control to prevent concurrency related problems, with the
help of an example. 10

(c) Consider the following Relations :
Employee (EName, EId, Addr I, Addr2, City, State) Works (EId, Branch, Dept_Name, Dept_No, Dept_Head)
Write the SQL statements for the following : 5
(i) Find all the ENames of employees who work in FINANCE department of Delhi Branch.
(ii) Find the Dept_Head for the employee if EName and EId are given.

4. (a) With the help of an example for each, explain Host Updates, Dirty Reads and Unrepeatable Reads of Concurrent transactions. 10

(b) Give the difference between operating system and database security. 5

(c) Explain the different forms of Authorization techniques. 5

5. Write short notes on the following : 4x5=20
(a) Any 4 Commands of DML
(b) Serialisable Schedules
(c) Data Replication in Distributed Databases
(d) 3-Tier Architecture

MCA (Revised)
Chapter 12: Term-End Examination, June, 2016
MCS-023: Database Management Systems

Time: 3 Hours
Maximum Marks: 100
Weightage: 70

Note: (i) Question No. 1 is compulsory.
(ii) Answer any three Questions from the rest.

1. (a) Consider the following three transactions :

T1	**T2**	**T3**
Read (X)	Read (X)	Read (X)
X = X —1000	display (X)	Y : = (X)
Write (X)		display (X)

Insert shared and exclusive locks in T 1 , **T2** and **T3** such that the transactions when executed concurrently, do not encounter
any concurrency problem. 10

(b) List all the functional dependencies that hold true for the following relation : 10

A	**B**	**C**
a_1	b_1	c_1
a_1	b_1	c_2
a_2	b_1	c_1
a_2	b_1	c_3

(c) Explain the working of GROUP BY clause. What is the difference between the WHERE and HAVING clause in SQL ?
5

(d) Differentiate between the following : 10
(1) Backward recovery and Forward recovery
(ii) Serial Schedule and Serializable Schedule

(e) Discuss the role of a Database Administrator. 5

2. (a) Construct an E-R diagram for the following problem definition : 8
Each company operates four departments, and each department belongs to one company. Each department employs one or
more employees, and each employee works for one department. Each of the employees may or may not have one or more
dependants, and each dependant belongs to one employee.

(b) What are the different types of constraints which can be imposed on Generalization in an E-R diagram ?

6

(c) How would you map the following E-R constructs into relations ? Give suitable examples. 6
(i) Aggregation
(ii) Inheritance
(iii) n-ary Relationship

3. (a) With the help of an example, explain client server databases. How are they different from distributed databases ?

10

(b) Consider the following relation for published books :
Book (Book_title, Author_name, Book_type, Listprice, Author_affil, Publisher)
Author_affil refers to the affiliation of the author. Suppose the following dependencies exist :
Book_title —> Publisher, Book_type
Book_type —> Listprice
Author_name --> Author_affil
(i) What Normal Form is the above relation in ? Justify.
(ii) Normalize the above relation till 3NF. 10

4. (a) Consider the following relations for a database that keeps a track of business trips of salespersons in a sales office :
SALEPERSON (SSN, Name, Start Year, Dept_No)
TRIP (SSN, From_City, To_City, Departure_Date, Return_Date, Trip_ID)
EXPENSE (Trip_ID, Account#, Amount)
Specify the queries in SQL.
(i) Find the details (all attributes of TRIP relation) for trips whose expenses exceeds $ 2000.
(ii) Find the SSN of salesmen who took trips to 'Honolulu'.
(iii) Find the total trip expenses incurred by the salesman with SSN = '234-56-7890'. 12

(b) Define a view. How is it different from a table ? Write the SQL syntax for creating a view. 8

5. (a) Discuss the different possible states of a transaction with the help of a diagram. 7

(b) Compare the shadow-paging recovery scheme with the log-based recovery scheme in respect to ease of implementation
and overhead cost. 8

(c) Discuss the key control measures that are used to provide security to data in databases. 5

MCA (Revised)
Chapter 13: Term-End Examination, December,2016
MCS-023: Database Management Systems

Time: 3 Hours
Maximum Marks: 100
Weightage: 70

Note: (i) Question No. 1 is compulsory.
(ii) Answer any three Questions from the rest.

1. (a) Compute the closure of the following set F of functional dependencies for relation schema R = (A, B, C, D, E).
A → BC
CD → E
B → D
E → A
List the candidate keys for R. 8

(b) Justify the following statements : 8
(i) Relation must have a key.
(ii) Weak entities do not have their own key attributes.

(c) Compare primary, secondary and clustering indexes. Which of these indexes are dense and which are not ? How is implementation of clustering indexes performed ? 10

(d) Consider the following relations :

A:

Pid	PName
001	abc
002	cde
011	efg
014	ghi
015	ijk
016	klm

B:

Pid	PName
002	cde
011	efg
015	ijk

016	klm

Find the following : 10
(i) A U B
(ii) A — B
(iii) A n B
(iv) A x B
(e) Explain briefly about Data Replication. Give its disadvantages. 4
2. (a) For the following problem definition :
The book club has members. The book club sells books to its members. The members place orders for books, which the book club fulfils. Each order contains one or more than one book. The books are written by author(s). The publisher publishes the book. An author can write more than one book and a book can have more than one author. A book is published by a publisher, but a publisher publishes many books. A member can place more than one order. The member also can choose not to place an order. The book club sells many books. Draw an ER Diagram. 10
(b) Consider the 'F' and `G' sets of functional dependencies, where
F = —> C, —> D, E --> AD, E 111 and G.{A—>CD,E—>AH}.
Check whether they are equivalent or not. 5
(c) Consider the relation R(A, B, C, D, E), and the set of functional dependencies F = D, {A, B} —> C, D —+ El.
Which of the following is a candidate key ? 5
(0 {A}
(ii) {A, BI
(iii) {A, El
3. (a) Consider the precedence graph of a schedule given below. Is the schedule conflict serializable ? Justify. 5

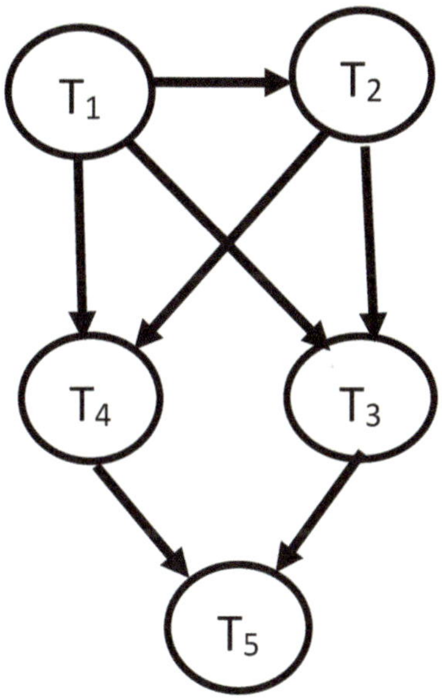

(b) Discuss the wait-die and wound-wait protocols for deadlock prevention. 7

(c) Distinguish between deferred update and immediate update log based recovery techniques. 8

4. (a) Consider the following tables :
WORKS(Pname, Cname, Salary)
LIVES(Pname, Street, City)
LOCATED(Cname, City)

MANAGER(Pname, Mname)

Write a query in SQL for the following : 10

(i) List the names of the people who work for the company Wipro' along with the cities they live in.

(ii) Find the people who work for the company `Infosys' having salary greater than 50,000.

(iii) List the names of the people, along with the street and city addresses.

(iv) Find the persons whose salaries are more than that of all of the 'Oracle' employees.

(v) Find the names of the persons who do not work in `Infosys'.

(b) Discuss the following relational constraints : 10

(i) Domain

(ii) Entity

(iii) Referential Integrity

(iv) Key Constraint

5. (a) Discuss the anomalies due to insertion, updation and deletion in a relation that is not in QNF. Illustrate with the help of an example. 5

(b) Write short notes on the following : 3x5=15

(i) Web Databases

(ii) Distributed Databases

(iii) Shadow Paging

MCA (Revised)
Chapter 14: Term-End Examination, June, 2017
MCS-023: Database Management Systems

Time: 3 Hours
Maximum Marks: 100
Weightage: 70

Note: (i) Question No. 1 is compulsory.
(ii) Answer any three Questions from the rest.

1. (a) Draw an ER diagram for the following situation :
"An academic institution is affiliated to a University. The institution possesses several departments, each department offers several courses. Each department has its own infrastructure, where several teachers teach several students." Transform your ER diagram into Relational Database.
10

(b) "Any relation in)3CNF is in 3NF, but the converse is not true." Justify the statement. 5

(c) Perform Union, Intersection and Set Difference Operation on the following relations R1 and R2 :
6

R_1

A	B
A_1	B_1
A_2	B_2
A_3	B_3
A_4	B_4

R_2

A	B
A_1	B_1
A_7	B_7
A_2	B_2
A_4	B_4

(d) Consider the Relational Database Schema given below :
Employee (empcode, empname, empaddress, salary)
Department (deptcode, deptname, deptlocation)
Perform the following queries using SQL and Relational Algebra : 5
(i) Find details of the departments located in Delhi.
(ii) Find the names of employees whose salary is more than 4 lakhs per annum.

(e) What are integrity constraints ? Discuss the various types of integrity constraints that can be imposed on databases.
5

(f) How are database security and database integrity related ? Briefly discuss the different levels of security measures which may be considered to protect the database. 5

(g) Compare and contrast the Distributed databases with the Centralised databases. 4

2. (a) With the help of a suitable example, discuss the insertion, deletion and updation anomalies that can occur in a database.
Briefly discuss the mechanism to remove such anomalies. 10

(b) What do you understand by the term 'Transaction' in a database ? Discuss the properties of the transactions and explain
the states through which a transaction passes during execution. 10

3. (a) Write SQL commands for each of the following. Also illustrate the usage of each command through suitable example.
10

(i) Creation of views
(ii) Creation of sequences
(iii) Outer join
(iv) To give access permission to any user

(b) Discuss the importance of file organisation in databases. Mention the different types of file organisations available. Discuss any one of the mentioned file organisations in detail. 10

4. (a) Perform the following tasks for the relation R(A, B, C, D, E) whose functional dependency set (FD) is given below :
FD: {AB —> C, C —> D, D —> A, BD —> E)
(i) Identify the candidate keys for the relation **(R).**
(ii) Identify the highest normal form possessed by the relation (R). Justify your answer.
(iii) Normalize the relation (R). 10

(b) For what reasons is 2-phase locking protocol required ? Explain. Discuss the disadvantages of basic 2-phase locking
protocol. List the ways and means that can be used to overcome the disadvantages. 10

5. Write short notes on any **four** of the following : 4x5=20
(a) Optimistic Scheduling
(b) 2-Phase Commit Protocol
(c) Indexed Sequential File Organisation
(d) Data Recovery Techniques
(e) Serializable Scheduling

MCA (Revised)
Chapter 15: Term-End Examination, December,2017
MCS-023: Database Management Systems

Time: 3 Hours
Maximum Marks: 100
Weightage: 70

Note: (i) Question No. 1 is compulsory.
(ii) Answer any three Questions from the rest.

1. (a) Draw an ER diagram for the situation given below :
"In a department many employees are working on many projects, which are under control of the manager of the department. The manager of the department also holds the responsibility of the welfare of the employees." Make suitable choices of the attributes for the entities, identified by you for your ER. diagram. Transform your ER diagram into a Relational Database. 10
(b) Which of the following functional dependencies holds for the . Relation (R) given below ? Justify your answer.
Relation (R) : 6

J	K	L
X	1	2
X	1	3
Y	1	4
Y	1	3
Z	2	5
P	4	7

Functional Dependencies :
(i) J --> K
(ii) K —> J
(iii) J, K —> L

(c) What is the role of views in DBMS ? Can we perform insert, delete or modify operations, if the view contains a group function ? Justify. 4

(d) Why do we do normalization of databases ? Discuss synthesis and decomposition approaches of normalization. Give one example for each approach. 5

(e) What is the significance of checkpoints in DBMS ? Discuss the utility of checkpoints, with the help of suitable example.
5

(f) Consider the following relational database schema :
Employer (ecode, ename, eaddress, esalary)
Project (pcode, pname, pduration)
Works for (ecode, pcode, duration)
Perform the following queries using SQL and relational algebra : 5
(i) Find the name of the employees whose salary is less than 5 lacs per annum.

(ii) Find the details of the employees working on the project "Clusters".

(g) Describe the utility of data replication in distributed DBMS. Briefly discuss the concept of complete and selective replication. 5

2. (a) Explain ANSI-SPARC 3 level architecture of DBMS. Discuss the languages associated at different levels. What are the different types of data independence involved at different levels ? 10

(b) Discuss the following :
(i) Lossless Decomposition
(ii) Dependency Preserving Decomposition
Give suitable examples in support of your discussion. 10

3. (a) Consider the concurrent schedule of Transactions T1 and T2, given below :

Schedule	**T_1**	**T_2**	**Sum**
T_1: Read (Sum)	Read (Sum)		500
T_1: Sum = Sum - 100	Sum = Sum - 100		
T_2: Read (Sum)		Read (Sum)	
T_2: Sum = Sum + 200		Sum = Sum + 200	
T_1: Write (Sum)	Write (Sum)		
T_2: Write (Sum)		Write (Sum)	

Referring to the schedule given above, answer the following questions with justification : 10
(i) Which property of transactions is violated ?
(ii) What is the final status of 'SUM' ?
(iii) Is the schedule serializable ?
(iv) Which problem in database is contributed by the schedule given ?

(b) What is the need of indices in a database system ? Mention the categories of indices available in a DBMS. Which data structure is suitable for creating indices and why ? 10

4. Differentiate between the following : 4x5=20
(a) DBMS and File base systems
(b) 2-Phase locking and 2-Phase commit
(c) DDBMS and Centralized DBMS
(d) Serial schedule and Serializable schedule

5. Write short notes on any four of the following : 4x5=20
(a) Write Ahead Log Protocol
(b) Clustering Indices
(c) Locks and its Types
(d) Deadlock Prevention Protocols
(e) Advantages and Disadvantages Distributed DBMS

MCA (Revised)
Chapter 16: Term-End Examination, June, 2018
MCS-023: Database Management Systems

Time: 3 Hours
Maximum Marks: 100
Weightage: 70

Note: (i) Question No. 1 is compulsory.
(ii) Answer any three Questions from the rest.

1. (a) Justify the statement "BCNF is stronger than 3NF" with the help of a suitable example. 5

(b) Why is data replication useful in DDBMS ? What do you understand by the term complete and selective replication ?
5

(c) How can system log be used for recovery when multiple concurrent transactions are going on ? Explain with the help of an example. 5

(d) What is the role of views in DBMS ? Can we perform delete, modify or insert operations, if the view contains group function ? Justify. 5

(e) What do you understand by the term "closure of any relation" ? How is closure used to determine key of relation ? Explain
with an example. 5

(f) Can we use Binary Search Tree (BST) for indexing ? Justify. 5

(g) What is Query Optimization ? Discuss the role of Relational Algebra in query optimization. 5

(h) What is a Database manager ? Explain the components of database manager with the help of a diagram.
5

2. (a) Explain ANSI SPARC 3 level architecture of DBMS, with the details of languages associated at different levels and the type of data independence in between different levels. Give suitable diagram in support of your explanation.
7

(b) Consider the relation SUPPLIER given below, where S# and P# are keys, the functional dependency set FD is FD = {S# P# -4 city, S# ---> city)

SUPPLIER

S#	**X**	**X**	**X**	**Y**	**Y**
P#	1	2	3	1	2
CITY	DELHI	DELHI	DELHI	GOA	GOA

Now, perform the following :
(i) Determine the highest normal form of the relation SUPPLIER. 2
(ii) Normalize the relation SUPPLIER to the next higher normal form.
(iii) Discuss the Deletion and Insertion anomalies, which can occur in the relation SUPPLIER. 2

(c) Construct an ER diagram for the loan management system of a finance company. Loans are given on the purchase of various items with different interest rates. The company keeps track of defaulters and takes appropriate steps against them. Make and state suitable assumptions (if any). 7

3. (a) What is a serializable schedule in concurrent transaction ? How does serializable schedule differ from serial schedule ? Give suitable example in support of your discussion. The problems of deadlock and starvation are addressed by which schedules respectively ? Justify. 7

(b) What is Write-Ahead log protocol ? How is this protocol utilized in database recovery process ? Discuss with suitable example. 5

(c) Discuss the term wait-for graph. What is the utility of wait-for graph in describing deadlocks ? Give suitable example in support of your discussion. 8

4. (a) Differentiate between the following : 10
(i) Two-phase locking vs Two-phase commit protocol
(ii) Wait-wound vs Wait-die protocol

(b) Discuss the term optimistic scheduling. How is this technique used to manage concurrent transactions in databases ? What is the difference between timestamping and optimistic scheduling ? Give suitable examples in support of your discussion. 10

5. Write short notes on the following : 4x5=20
(a) Distributed DBMS
(b) Clustering Indexes and their Implementation
(c) Shadow Paging
(d) Weak Entity along with an example.
(e) Specialisation in ERD with an appropriate example.

MCA (Revised)
Chapter 17: Term-End Examination, December,2018
MCS-023: Database Management Systems

Time: 3 Hours
Maximum Marks: 100
Weightage: 70

Note: (i) Question No. 1 is compulsory.
(ii) Answer any three Questions from the rest.

1. (a) For the relations given below, check whether the given functional dependencies hold or not. Give proper justification.
5

J	X	X	Y	Y	Z	P
K	1	1	1	1	2	4
L	2	3	4	3	5	7

(i) J —> K
(ii) J, K —> L

(b) Verify the statement, "Any relation in BCNF is in 3NF but converse is not true." Give suitable example.
5

(c) Explain the term data replication and data fragmentation with suitable example. 5

(d) What are integrity constraints ? Explain the various types of integrity constraints with suitable examples.
5

(e) How do you implement a hierarchical data model ? Explain through an illustration. 5

(f) Define Data Manipulation Language (DML) of SQL. List and explain various DML commands.
5

(g) How do B-tree indexes differ from Binary search tree indexes ? 5

(h) Differentiate between the concepts of Logical data independence and . Physical data independence in DBMS.
5

2. (a) Draw an ER diagram for an open university system covering all the functionalities and also derive corresponding relational schema. 10
Note : Assumptions can be made wherever necessary. However, state them.

(b) What do you understand by the term closure of a relation (R) with functional dependency set (F) ? Compute the closure
for relation R(/, m, n, o, p) with functional dependency set F as given below :
F{/ —> mn; no —> p; m —> o; p l}
Identify the candidate keys for the relation (R). 10

3. (a) What do you understand by the term Query Optimization ? Discuss the role of relational algebra in Query Optimization.
List the operators used in relational algebra and discuss the operation of each, with suitable example.
10

(b) What is the need of indexes in DBMS ? Compare primary; secondary and clustering indexes. Which of these indexes are dense ? Give steps to perform implementation of clustering indexes. 10

4. (a) Explain the following with the help of an example : 8

(i) Integrity constraints and its types

(ii) Deadlock and its prevention in DBMS

(b) What are checkpoints ? How does this technique of checkpoints contribute to database recovery ? Give suitable example.

5

(c) What do you understand by the terms Lossless decomposition and Dependency Preserving decomposition ? Is it always

true that a lossless decomposition is dependency preserving too ? Give suitable example in support of your answer.

7

5. Write short notes on the following : 5x4=20

(a) Wait-for Graph

(b) Wait and Wound Protocol

(c) Two-Phase Locking Protocol

(d) Two-Phase Commit Protocol

(e) Data Replication in DDBMS

MCA (Revised)
Chapter 18: Term-End Examination, June, 2019
MCS-023: Database Management Systems

Time: 3 Hours
Maximum Marks: 100
Weightage: 70

Note: (i) Question No. 1 is compulsory.
(ii) Answer any three Questions from the rest.

1. (a) Consider the following relation which keeps records of employees joining and leaving the projects. Employee can work on many projects :
Project (emp_id emp_name, project_id, project_name, joining_date, leaving_date)
(i) What are the anamolies in the relation above ? Explain with examples. [6]
(ii) What are the functional dependencies in the relation ? [4]
(iii) Normalize the above relation into 2NF [5]

(b) Which precedence graph for the following schedule is correct ? State whether the schedule is serializable or out : [5]

Here is the same content and values based on the image provided:

Schedule	T_1	T_2
Read X	Read X	-
Add 500	Add 500	-
Read X	-	Read X
Write X	Write X	-
Read Y	-	Read Y
Read Y	Read Y	-
Subtract 200	Subtract 200	-
Display X+Y	-	Display X+Y
Write Y	Write Y	-

(i) $T_1 \rightarrow T_2$
(ii) $T_1 \leftarrow T_2$
(iii) $T_1 \leftrightarrow T_2$

(c) Consider the following relational schema: [4]
Student (Student_ID, student_name, program)
Course (Course_ID, Course_name, school_of studies)
Taught (Student_ID, Course_ID, Year, Instructor ID)
Write SQL statements for the following :
To retrieve the names of all 3rd year students of MCA Program who have done courses under Instructor ID-001 (ii) To retrieve the names of all courses taught by instructor-002 between 1996-2001 and total number of students attended the
courses.

(d) Explain wound-wait scheme for deadlock prevention with the help of an example. [6]

(e) How do we implement "B-Trees" as an Index ? Give an example to illustrate. What are its advantages ? [5]

(f) Explain the concept of a simple authorization with the help of an example. [5]

2. (a) Consider the relation between R, and **R2** and use them to preform the operations given below : 6

R_1

A	**B**
A_1	B_1
A_2	B_2
A_3	B_3
A_4	B_4

R_2

A	**B**
A_1	B_1
A_7	B_7
A_2	B_2
A_4	B_4

(i) $R_1 \cap R_2$
(ii) $R_1 — R_2$
(iii) $R_2 - R_1$

(b) Design an E-R diagram for a Bank database schema for the following statement : [5]
"Each bank can have multiple branches and each branch can have multiple accounts and loans." Convert the diagram into tables.

(c) Differentiate between the Basic 2PL and Strict 2PL with respect to atomicity, concurrency and deadlock. [7]

(d) What are the advantages of a view ? What are its limitations with respect to applying DM_2 operations ? [5]

3. (a) What is the dependency preservation property for a decomposition ? Why is it important ? [6]

(b) How do we recover from a transaction failure using "log" ? Illustrate through an example. [10]

(c) Differentiate between centralised databases and distributed databases. [4]

4. (a) What is a system log ? What are the typical kinds of entries in a system log ? [5]

(b) Describe the benefits of data replication in DDBMS. What typical units of data are replicated in the process of data
replications ? [5]

(c) Explain any two problems of concurrent transactions with the help of an example. [6]

(d) Prove the statement "Any relation which is in BCNF is in 3NF but the converse is not true". [4]

5. (a) With the help of an example, explain the process of vertical fragmentation. [6]

(b) Discuss the optimistic concurrency control with the help of an example. [8]

(c) How does a checkpoint mechanism help in database recovery ? Explain through an example. [6]

(d) Prove the statement "Any relation which is in BCNF is in 3NF but the converse is not true". [4]

MCA (Revised)
Chapter 19: Term-End Examination, December,2019
MCS-023: Database Management Systems

Time: 3 Hours
Maximum Marks: 100
Weightage: 70

Note: (i) Question No. 1 is compulsory.
(ii) Answer any three Questions from the rest.

1. (a) Define 2NF. How would you normalize the empproject relational scheme into 2NF. Emp-Project (SSN, P_number, hours, e_name, P-name, Plocation). [6]
where :
[SSN, p _ number] --> hours
SSN e _ name
p _number —>[p _name, p _location]

(b) XYZ bank manages four types of accounts : Loan, Current/Saving, Recurring and Deposits. It operates number of branches and a customer of the bank can have any number of accounts : [5]
(i) Identify entities of your interest, attributes, relationship, cardinalities and draw a complete E-R diagram.
(ii) Convert the E-R diagram into tables and show relationship among the tables as per the diagram. [5]

(c) Explain the two integrity rules with the help of an example for each. [5]

(d) Define a serializable schedule. For the following schedule (schedule A). Determine whether "schedule A" is serializable or not. [5]

T1	T2
Read (x)	-
-	Read(x)
Write (y)	-
-	Write (y)
Commit	-
-	Commit

(e) Explain database recovery using a system log with the help of an example. [6]

(f) What is a hashed file organization ? What are its advantages and disadvantages ? [5]

(g) For what reasons is '2-phase' locking protocol required ? [3]

2. (a) What types of constraints violation take place during insert operation ? Explain with an example. [5]

(b) What is the difference between a key and a super key ? Define primary key, candidate key and foreign key. [5]

(c) Violation of which property of a transaction leads to lost-update problem ? Explain with a suitable example. [6]

(d) Explain the meanings of the following clauses with appropriate example for each : [4]

(i) Group by clause
(ii) Having clause

3. (a) What is a binary lock ? How does it solve a concurrency related problem ? Explain through an example. [7]

(b) What are the reasons for fragmenting a relation ? What are the rules to be applied for fragmenting a relation ? [5]

(c) What is a weak-entity ? What are the restrictions on weak entity ? Explain through an example.[5]

(d) Differentiate between data . security and data integrity. [3]

4. (a) Compare the shadow-page recovery technique with log-based recovery technique with respect to ease of implementation and overhead cost. [6]

(b) What is a data dictionary ? What should be included in data dictionary ? [5]

(c) What do you mean by ALTER TABLE command ? Write its syntax in any four possible situations where it is used. [5]

(d) What is a B+ tree ? Why is a 13+ tree better structure than a B-Tree for implementation of an index sequential file ? [4]

5. (a) What is a precedence graph ? Why it is used ? Write all the steps for constructing a precedence graph. [6]

(b) (i) Differentiate between backward recovery and forward recovery. [4]
(ii) What is a key advantage of checkpoint recovery mechanism ? [2]

(c) With the help of a suitable example, explain inverted file organisation. [4]

(d) Discuss any two levels of security mechanisms to protect database. [4]

MCA (Revised)
Chapter 20: Term-End Examination, June, 2020
MCS-023: Database Management Systems

Time: 3 Hours
Maximum Marks: 100
Weightage: 70

Note: (i) Question No. 1 is compulsory.
(ii) Answer any three Questions from the rest.

1. (a) Explain ANSI SPARC 3 level architecture of logical DBMS. What is the need for the three level architecture ? 5

(b) Describe the relationship between Data Security and Data Integrity, with the help of a diagram. 5

(c) Explain the terms BCNF and 3NF and verify the statement "any relation in BCNF is in 3NF but converse is not true." 5

(d) What do you understand by the term "data replication" ? Why is data replication useful in DDBMS ? Briefly discuss complete and selective replication. 5

(e) Draw an E-R diagram of a manufacturing company that makes various kinds of products. The company has several customers. Some of whom have offices inmultiple locations. The customers place the order on the company for shopping products to different offices. Assume reasonable attributes for the entities. 5

(f) What are integrity constraints ? What for they are required in databases ? Briefly discuss the different types of integrity constraints. 5

(g) What are Indexes in DBMS ? What is the utility of Indexes in DBMS ? Under what situations B-tree Indexes are preferrable over Binary Search Tree Indexes ? 5

(h) What is the difference between strong and weak entities ? Specify strong and weak, entities in the above E-R diagram. 5

2. (a) What do you understand by the term "Normalization" in DBMS ? Write statement for second normal form (2NF), and discuss the insert, delete and update anomalies associated with 2 NF. 10

(b) What are concurrent transactions ? Briefly discuss the problems encountered by concurrent transactions. 10

3. (a) What is Relational Algebra ? What is the utility of relational algebra ? Is SQL related to relational algebra ? Comment on it. Explain the following operations in the relational algebra with the help of an example for each : 10

(i) Select
(ii) Project
(iii) Join

(b) What is the role of Database Manager ? Explain the important components of database manager with the help of a diagram. 10

4. (a) What do you understand by the term functional dependency ? Explain the following functional dependencies : 10

(i) Full functional dependency
(ii) Partial functional dependency
(iii) Transitive functional dependency
(iv) Trivial functional dependency

(b) Explain the following terms with suitable example : 10
(i) Lossless decomposition
(ii) Dependency preserving decomposition

5. Write short notes on the following : 20
(i) 2-Phase locking protocol
(ii) 2-Phase commit protocol
(iii) Time-stamping protocol
(iv) Checkpoints

MCA (Revised)
Chapter 22: Term-End Examination, February,2021
MCS-023: Database Management Systems

Time: 3 Hours
Maximum Marks: 100
Weightage: 70

Note: (i) Question No. 1 is compulsory.
(ii) Answer any three Questions from the rest.

1. (a) Determine the output when the following operations are applied on Relation R1, R2 and R3 given below : 5

R_1:

A	B
a_1	b_1
a_2	b_2
a_3	b_3
a_4	b_4

R_2:

A	B
a_1	b_1
a_7	b_7
a_2	b_2
a_4	b_4

A
Empty

(i) Union (R1 U R2)
(ii) Intersection (R1 ∩ R2)
(iii) Difference ($R_1 - R_2$)
(iv) Cartesian Cross Section (R_1 X R_2)
(v) Division (R_1 / R_3)

(b) How do weak entities differ from strong entities ? Discuss with the help of an example. Briefly discuss the role of keys in identification of the entity type, i.e. weak or strong. 5

(c) What do you understand by functional dependency in a Relational DBMS ? For the relation given below, check whether the given functional dependencies hold or not. Give proper justification. 5

J	K	L
x	1	2
x	1	3
y	1	4
y	1	3
z	2	5
p	4	7

(i) J → K
(ii) K → J
(iii) J, K → L
(iv) K, L → J

(d) List the properties of concurrent transactions. Consider the concurrent schedule of the transactions T1 and T2 given below :

Schedule	T_1	T_2	Sum
T1:Read(Sum)	Read(Sum)		500
T1:Sum=Sum−100	Sum = Sum - 100		
T2:Read(Sum)		Read(Sum)	
T2:Sum=Sum+500		Sum = Sum + 500	
T1:Write(Sum)	Write(Sum)		
T2:Write(Sum)		Write(Sum)	

Referring to the schedule above, answer the following questions : 5
(i) Which property of transaction is violated ?
(ii) Identify the final status of sum.
(iii) The given schedule contributes to which problem in databases ?

(e) What are the advantages and disadvantages of distributed databases ? 5

(f) What is the difference between DBMS and RDBMS ? Under what situations is it better to use File-based System than
Database System ? 5

(g) Explain database recovery using system log with the help of an example. 5

(h) Explain the following terms : 5
(i) Candidate key
(ii) Primary key
(iii) Foreign key
(iv) Super key
(v) Alternate key

2. (a) What are checkpoints ? Discuss the role of checkpoints in database recovery. Give suitable example in support of your
discussion. 10

(b) Explain 3NF. Discuss the Insert, Delete and Update anomalies associated with 3NF. 10

3. Differentiate the following : 20
(i) Centralized and Distributed DBMS
(ii) Deadlock avoidance and Deadlock prevention protocols
(iii) 2 Phase locking and 2 Phase commit
(iv) 3NF and BCNF

4. Write short notes on following : 20
(i) Precedence graph for serializability check
(ii) Types of Indexes in DBMS
(iii) Data fragmentation and its objectives
(iv) Problems of serial schedule and serializable schedule

5. (a) Can we use Binary Search Tree (BST) as Indexes ? Justify. If we use BST as Index, then what can be the possible problems ? What will be the solution for those problems ? 10

(b) Consider ''Library Management System'' which keeps the following tables :
Book (isbn_no, title, author, publisher, edition, year)
Book_Access (access_no, isbn_no, date_of_purchase)
Member (m_name, m_id, m_address, m_phone)
Issue_Return (access_no, m_id, expected_return_date, actual_return_date)
Specify the following queries in SQL : 10
(i) Find m_id and m_name of the members who have got at least one book issued to themselves.
(ii) List the book details for the books which were purchased after January 2017.
(iii) List all the books on title ''Databases''. This list should be sorted on author's name.
(iv) Find the members who have not got any book issued.

MCA (Revised)
Chapter 23: Term-End Examination, June, 2021
MCS-023: Database Management Systems

Time: 3 Hours
Maximum Marks: 100
Weightage: 70

Note: (i) Question No. 1 is compulsory.
(ii) Answer any three Questions from the rest.

1. (a) What are integrity constraints ? Discuss the entity integrity and referential integrity constraints with suitable example. 5

(b) Explain the three-level architecture of DBMS with the help of a diagram. 5

(c) Explain the concept 3rd normal form with the help of an example. 5

(d) Consider the following three tables : 10
student (student_id, name, date_of_birth)
registers ((student_id, course_id)
course (course_id, course_title, credits)
Write the SQL commands for the following queries :
(i) List all the courses in alphabetical order of course title.
(ii) Make a list of students who have registered for course whose course_id is "MCS-23".
(iii) Count the total number of students in each course.
(iv) List all the courses whose credits are less than 4.
(v) List all the students who have registered for more than one course.

(e) What is a transaction in the context of DBMS ? Explain the properties of a transaction with the help of an example. 7

(f) Differentiate between primary and secondary indexes in the context of file organisation. 3

(g) Describe the utility of data replication in distributed DBMS with the help of an example. 5

2. (a) Draw an ER diagram for the situation given below : 10
"A company has many employees, working on several projects. A project is controlled by a manager who is an employee of the company." Perform the following tasks for the description given above :
(i) Identify entities, attributes, relationships, cardinalities, and draw an ER diagram.
(ii) Convert the ER diagram into tables and show relationship among the tables as per the ER diagram.

(b) Describe the relationship between data security and data integrity, with the help of a diagram. 5

(c) Compare strong and weak entities in the context of ER diagram with the help of an example. 5

3. (a) What are concurrent transactions ? Briefly discuss the problems encountered by concurrent transactions. 10

(b) Briefly discuss the term normalization in DBMS. Write statement for Second Normal Form (2NF) and discuss the insert, delete and update anomalies associated with 2NF. 10

4. (a) Explain database recovery using system log, with the help of an example. Compare the backward recovery with forward
recovery with the help of an example of each. 10

(b) Discuss the role of database manager of a DBMS. Draw diagram to show the important components of database manager. Explain the role of each component shown in the diagram. 10

5. Explain any **five** of the following : 5×4=20

(a) 2-phase locking protocol
(b) Deadlock prevention protocol
(c) Data fragmentation in DDBMS
(d) Cartesian product and division operations in relational algebra
(e) Inverted file organisation
(f) Client-server databases

MCA (Revised)
Chapter 24: Term-End Examination, December,2021
MCS-023: Database Management Systems

Time: 3 Hours
Maximum Marks: 100
Weightage: 70

Note: (i) Question No. 1 is compulsory.
(ii) Answer any three Questions from the rest.

1. (a) Consider the following two relations :
Customer and Sales_order :
Customer and Sales_order:

Customer

Cust_No	Name	Address
C10	N1	AD1
C11	N2	AD2

Sales_order

Order_No	Date	Cust_No
OD10	1/6/19	C10
OD11	1/7/19	NULL
OD12	11/7/19	C12
NULL	1/8/19	C11

The underlined attributes are primary keys. State with proper reasoning which, if any, of the entity integrity rules are violated for each of the above tuples (row) in Sales_order relation. 8

(b) Define the serializable schedule. State with proper explanation whether the following schedule is serializable or not :
6

T1	T2
read(X);	
	read(X);
write(Y);	
	write(Y);
commit	
	commit

(c) Define 2NF. The following are the functional dependencies in a relation :
(order_no, item_code) → primary key
item_code → price/unit
order_no → order_date
Is this relation in 2NF ? Justify. In case the relation is not in 2NF, convert it in 2NF. 8

(d) Consider the following relations in a database that maintains the official tours of sales executives in a marketing company.
Sales_Executive (SEID, Dept_No, Joining_year)
Official_Tour (Tour_ID, from_city, to_city,
dep_date, ret_date, SEID)
Expenditure (Tour_ID, Amt_spent)

Write the queries using SQL : 6

(i) Find the details of Official_Tour relation whose expenses exceed < 5000.

(ii) Find the total official tour expenses incurred by sales executives from Dept_No = DN1.

(iii) Find the SEID's of sales executives who took trips to Bangalore for seven days with expenses ranging between < 5000 and < 9000.

(e) An academic organization has a student entity set which can be of two types — Full time and Part time as shown below:

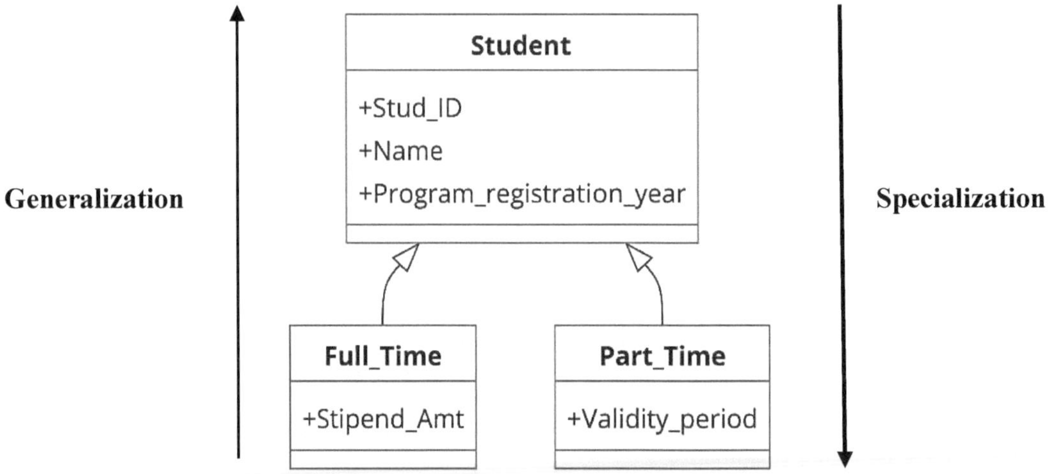

Figure : Generalization/Specialization Hierarchy Convert the above diagram into tables. 6

(f) What are the two advantages of a B-Tree as an index ? Write the important features of B-Tree of order N. 6

2. (a) Define a view. Explain with the help of an example. Also specify the conditions that a view must meet in order to allow updates. 8

(b) Identify the following symbols in relational algebra. What operations do they perform ? 4

(i) σ

(ii) π

(c) Consider the following relation Person :

Person

P-ID	**Name**	**Age**	**Salary**
P-ID1	Ram	20	15000.00
P-ID2	Shyam	25	25000.00
P-ID3	Sita	30	30000.00
P-ID4	Gita	35	35000.00

What will be the output of the following operations on the Person relation ? 4

(i) σ > = 25 (Person)

(ii) π age, salary (Person)

(d) Where are Having and Group by clauses used ? What will be the output of the following SQL statement on the Person relation defined above in Q. no. 2(c) ? 4

Select Name, Max (Salary)

From Person

Group by Name Having Max (Salary) > 15000

3. (a) With the help of an example for each, explain the following : 2x3=6

(i) Binary Lock

(ii) Multiple-mode Locks

b) Define primary and clustering indexes. Briefly discuss implementation of clustering indexes. 8

(c) Discuss the advantages and disadvantages of data replication. What are the objectives of complete and selective replication ? 6

4. (a) What is use of a precedence graph in database ? Write all the steps for constructing a precedence graph. Suppose there are two transactions T1 and T2. Draw an edge between T1 and T2, if T2 has written on item X first and T1 writes on the same item later. 10

(b) What is Log-Based Recovery System ? Explain the type of information kept in a log about transaction. Which type of transactions are selected for REDO and UNDO for database recovery ? Explain with an example. 10

5. (a) Describe the following client-server architecture with the help of a diagram : 2x5=10

(i) 2-tier

(ii) 3-tier

(b) Explain the following concepts with the help of suitable example : 2x5=10

(i) Lossless decomposition

(ii) Dependency preserving decomposition

MCA (Revised)
Chapter 25: Term-End Examination, June, 2022
MCS-023: Database Management Systems

Time: 3 Hours
Maximum Marks: 100
Weightage: 70

Note: (i) Question No. 1 is compulsory.
(ii) Answer any three Questions from the rest.

1. (a) Draw ANSI-SPARC 3-level architecture of DBMS. Write the languages associated with different levels of ANSI-SPARC 3-level architecture. 5

(b) In terms of DBMS, what is a transaction ? Discuss ACID properties of transaction. 5

(c) Compare and contrast serial file organization technique with indexed sequential technique in terms of storage, access and other features. 5

(d) Define a JOIN operation, How is this different from Cartesian product in relational algebra ? Explain with the help of an example. 5

(e) Compare BCNF and 3NF. Discuss insert, delete and update anomalies in 3NF, with a suitable example of each. 10

(f) Discuss the role of views in DBMS ? Can we perform insert, delete or modify operations, if the view contains a group function ? Justify. 5

(g) Explain the terms data replication and data fragmentation, with the help of a suitable example. 5

2. (a) Create an ER diagram for ''LOAN MANAGEMENT SYSTEM'' of a finance company. The company offers various kinds of loans like Personal loans, Vehicle loans, Home loans, Marriage loans, etc. To avail them, they had put some criteria as well as need for submission of support documents. Various loans come with variable interest rates. The company keeps track of all the customers whether they are paying regularly or not. It tracks defaulters and takes appropriate steps to recover the loan/instalments. Make and state suitable assumptions (if any). 10

(b) What do you understand by Query Optimization in DBMS ? How does relational algebra help in Optimizing the Query ? Discuss with suitable example. List the operators used in relational algebra and briefly explain them. 10

3. (a) What is Normalization ? Compare the Synthesis and Decomposition approach of Normalization. Discuss Lossless decomposition and Dependency preserving decomposition, with a suitable example of each. 10

(b) What are Checkpoints ? How does this technique of Checkpoints contribute to database recovery ? 4

(c) Consider the following schema :
Employee (ENo, EName, City, Basic_Sal, Job_Status)
Projects (PNo, PName, PCategory)
Works_In (PNo, ENo, PDuration)
Write the appropriate SQL queries for the following : 3x2=6
(i) Display all the names of the employees who are working in ''PAY_ROLL FOR ABC COMPANY'' project.
(ii) Display the ENo, EName of all the employees who are working in PNo = 123.

(iii) Find the average salary of all the employees working in a project with PName ''ADMINISTRATION MODULE OF XYZ'' Company.

4. Differentiate between the following (give example for each) : 4x5=20

(a) Client-Server vs. Distributed Database
(b) Centralized DBMS vs. Distributed DBMS
(c) DBMS vs. File Base Systems
(d) 2-Phase Locking vs. 2-Phase Commit

5. Write short notes on the following : 4x5=20

(a) Concurrent Transactions
(b) Hashed File Organization
(c) DML Commands used in DBMS (any four)
(d) Functional Dependency

MCA (Revised)
Chapter 26: Term-End Examination, December,2022
MCS-023: Database Management Systems

Time: 3 Hours
Maximum Marks: 100
Weightage: 70

Note: (i) Question No. 1 is compulsory.
(ii) Answer any three Questions from the rest.

1. (a) State the two integrity rules. In the following two relations : customer and sales-order, state which if any, of the integrity rules are violated, when the following tuples (rows) from (i) to (iv) are added to the sales-order relation : 8

Customer

Cust- No	Name	Address
C15	NM-1	ADR-1
C16	NM-2	ADR-2

Sales-Order

Order No	Date	Cust-No

(i) <013, 2/6/2019, C15>
(ii) <014, 3/6/2019, NULL>
(iii) <015, 4/6/2019, C17>
(iv) <Null, 5/6/2019, C16>
The underlined attributes are primary keys in the above relations.

(b) Is the following schedule serializable ? Explain. 6

Here is the content from the image you uploaded, structured as shown:

T1	T2
read(X);	
	write(X);
read(X);	
write(Y);	
Commit	
	Commit

(c) Define 3NF. Justify whether the following employee relation is in 3NF or not : 6
employee (emp_code, emp_name, deptt, salary, project_no, termination_date)
where Project_No. →termination_date. The underlined attribute is PK. If it is not in 3NF, convert it into 3NF.

(d) Consider the following relatives :
Student (Stdid, Std_name, year_of_study, basic_stipend, dept_no.)
dept. (dept_no, dept_name, academic_block)
write SQL queries for the following : 6

(i) List std_name year_of_study, dept_name of all students whose name starts with "K".
(ii) Select names of all the students of Computer Science dept_name whose basic stipend is more than ` 8,000 per month.
(iii) Increase the basic stipend of 3rd-year engineering dept. by ` 3,000 per month.

(e) Design an E-R diagram for the following and also create its related tables : 6
"A faculty can teach many courses and a course can be taught by many faculty members."

(f) What are the different file organization techniques based on access key ? Describe the implementation mechanism for each technique. 4

(g) What are the rules to be followed for fragmenting the relation ? Create two horizontal fragments frag 1 and frag 2 on
the state attribute Delhi and Haryana respectively of deposit relation given below. How are the horizontal fragments specified through algebraic operations ? 4

Deposit Relation

State	Acc_No.	Cust_Name	Deposit_Amt
Delhi	ACC 1	CN 1	5,000.00
Delhi	ACC 2	CN 2	10,000.00
Delhi	ACC 3	CN 1	6,000.00
Haryana	ACC 4	CN 2	15,000.00
Delhi	ACC 5	CN 4	12,000.00
Haryana	ACC 6	CN 4	15,000.00
Haryana	ACC 7	CN 2	25,000.00

2. (a) What will be the result of the following algebraic operations on the following relations R1 and R2 ? 6

(i) R1 ∪ R2
(ii) R1 ∩ R2

Table R1:

E_id	E_name
Eid1	N1
Eid2	N2
Eid3	N3
Eid4	N4
Eid5	N5

Table R2:

E_id	E_name
Eid2	N2
Eid4	N4
Eid5	N5

(b) What are order by clause and aggregate functions in SQL ? Consider the employee table having the following tuples :

ID	EName	Salary (`)	Age	Department
ID1	N1	20,000	30	D1

ID2	N2	15,000	35	D2
ID 3	N3	25,000	40	D2
ID 4	N4	30,000	35	D3
ID 5	N5	22,000	45	D4
ID 6	N6	27,000	42	D4

What will be the result of the following query from the above employee table of Q. 2(b) ? 6+2

(i) Select from employee ORDER by Salary Name.

(ii) Select Max (salary) from employee.

(iii) Select Avg (age) from employee.

(c) What are the advantages of having three levels of database architectures ? How are they related to data independence ? Discuss. 6

3. (a) Define primary, secondary and foreign keys. Identify the primary and foreign keys in the following relations : Students and School of studies : 6

Table: Student

Std_ID	Program	Department
ID1	M. C. A.	D1
ID2	M. C. A.	D1
ID3	B. Sc.	D2
ID4	M. A.	D3

Table: School of Studies

Department	Name	Location
D1	Computer Science	C-Block
D2	Science	D-Block
D3	Social Science	F-Block

(b) Explain the meaning of the following two keywords :
Commit and Rollback. Write a code fragment for transferring money from account A to account B and show the uses of Commit and Rollback. Assume both accounts A and B exist in the bank. 6

(c) What are the reasons for occurrences of a deadlock in a database system ? Explain how does wait die scheme prevent in deadlock. Explain with the help of an example. 8

4. (a) (i) What is the use of locks in allowing multiple transactions running concurrently ? Why are multiple-mode locks preferable over a binary lock ? The following is a schedule with the initial values of X and Y are 50 and 60 respectively :

4

Schedule

No	T1	T2
1	LOCK X	
2	LOCK Y	

3	READ X	
4	X = X + 50	
5	Write X	
6	Unlock X	
7		Lock X
8		Lock Y
9	READ T	
10	Y = Y - 40	
11	Write Y	
12	UNLOCK Y	
13		READ X
14		READ Y
15		Output = X + Y
16		Display Output
17		UNLOCK X
18		UNLOCK Y

Answer the following questions :
(ii) Whether the schedule is serializable or not ? Justify. 4
(iii) What will be the output value (schedule 16) ? 2
(iv) Whether the schedule Nos. 7 and 8 will be granted or not ? 2

(b) Discuss the basic model of database access control with the help of the following example : 8
Student (stdid, Name, e-mail, stipend, grade)
Assume that there are two types of users : student administrator and a student. Create a sample authorization matrix for the above relation.

5. (a) Write SQL commands for each of the following. Also illustrate the usage of each command : 10
(i) Creation of sequences
(ii) Outer Join
(iii) Creating views with check option
(iv) Database access permission to users

(b) State BCNF. What are the anomalies associated with a relation that is not in BCNF ? Why is BCNF considered stronger
than 3NF ? Discuss with a suitable example. 10

MCA (Revised)
Chapter 27: Term-End Examination, June, 2023
MCS-023: Database Management Systems

Time: 3 Hours
Maximum Marks: 100
Weightage: 70

Note: (i) Question No. 1 is compulsory.
(ii) Answer any three Questions from the rest.

1. (a) Compare File Base System with Database Management System. 5

(b) Why is data replication useful in Distributed Database Management System (DDBMS) ? Briefly discuss the terms „Complete Replication" and „Selective Replication". 5

(c) Briefly discuss the lost update problem with the help of a suitable example. 5

(d) Justify the statement "BCNF is stronger than 3NF". Give suitable example in support of your justification. 5

(e) What is Query Optimization ? Discuss the role of relational algebra in Query Optimization. 5

(f) What are integrity constraints ? Explain the various types of integrity constraints. 5

(g) How do strong entities differ from weak entities ? Discuss with the help of an example. Briefly discuss the role of keys
in identification of entity type (i.e. weak and strong). 5

(h) Discuss the role of Database Administration. 5

2. (a) Differentiate between serial schedule and serializable schedule. 5

(b) Compare primary, secondary and clustering indexes. Which of these indexes are dense and which are not ? How is implementation of clustering indexes performed ? 10

(c) Explain log based recovery scheme with the help of an example. 5

3. (a) What do you understand by the term „Normalization" in DBMS ? Write statement for second normal form (2NF), and discuss the insert, delete and update anomalies associated with 2NF. 10

(b) What do you understand by the term „functional dependency" ? Explain the following functional dependencies, with suitable example for each : 10
(i) Full functional dependency
(ii) Partial functional dependency
(iii) Transitive functional dependency
(iv) Trivial functional dependency

4. (a) Compare shadow paging recovery scheme with the log-based recovery scheme in respect of ease of implementation and overhead cost. 8

(b) Discuss different possible states of a transaction with the help of a diagram. 7

(c) Discuss the utility of data replication and data fragmentation in Distributed Databases. 5

5. Write short notes on the following : 5×4=20

(a) Deadlock prevention protocols

(b) Precedence graph for serializability check

(c) 2-tier client/server model

(d) Integrity constraints and its types

MCA (Revised)
Chapter 28: Term-End Examination, December,2023
MCS-023: Database Management Systems

Time: 3 Hours
Maximum Marks: 100
Weightage: 70

Note: (i) Question No. 1 is compulsory.
(ii) Answer any three Questions from the rest.

1. (a) Justify the statement "Any relation in BCNF is in 3NF but converse is not true." Support your answer with the help of an example. 5

(b) Compare object based data models with the record based logical data models. 5

(c) Briefly discuss the dirty read problem of DBMS with the help of a suitable example. 5

(d) Can we use Binary Search Trees (BST) for the purpose of indexing ? Justify. 5

(e) How do B-tree indexes differ from Binary search tree indexes ? 5

(f) Differentiate between logical data independence and physical data independence. 5

(g) Describe the relationship between data security and data integrity, with the help of a diagram. 5

(h) Differentiate between DBMS and RDBMS. Under what situation is it better to use file base system than database system?
5

2. (a) Differentiate between Backward recovery and Forward recovery. 5

(b) Define a view in SQL. How does it differ from a table ? Write SQL syntax for creating a view. 5

(c) What is conflict serializability ? Explain. Consider the precedence graph of a schedule given below. Is the schedule conflict serializable ? Justify. 10

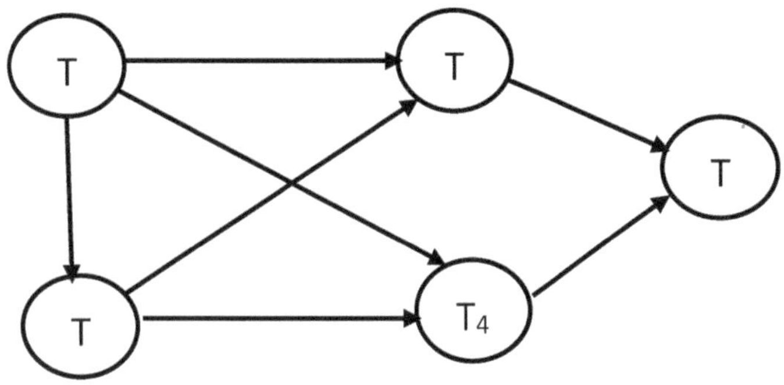

3. (a) Explain the concept of lossless decomposition and dependency preserving decomposition with suitable example for each. Is it always true that a lossless decomposition is dependency preserving too ? Justify with suitable example.
10

(b) What is Relational Algebra ? What is the utility of Relational Algebra ? Is SQL related to Relational Algebra ? Comment on it. Explain the following operations in the relational algebra with the help of an example for each : 10

(i) Select
(ii) Project
(iii) Join

4. (a) Discuss the term optimistic scheduling. How is this technique used to manage concurrent transactions in databases ? How does it differ from time stamping ? Give suitable example in support of your discussion. 10

(b) Differentiate between the following : 5 each
(i) Two-phase locking protocol and Two-phase commit protocol
(ii) Wait-wound protocol and Wait-die protocol

5. Write short notes on the following : 4×5=20
(a) Deadlock avoidance protocols
(b) Data fragmentation and its objectives
(c) Problems of serial schedule and serializable schedule
(d) Properties of Transactions in DBMS